Perspectives

Holiday Destinations
Are They Overloved?

T0359737

Flying Start
to Literacy®

Contents

Introduction

How do we protect our holiday destinations from too many visitors?

Beautiful places are often popular holiday destinations and they can be inundated by visitors! Some of these visitors spend money and this helps the local people.

But if there are too many visitors, they can cause problems. They may be noisy and intrusive, or they might damage natural attractions.

Who has the greatest rights – the locals who live there or the visitors? Do travellers have the right to go wherever they want? How can popular holiday destinations be protected but still welcome visitors?

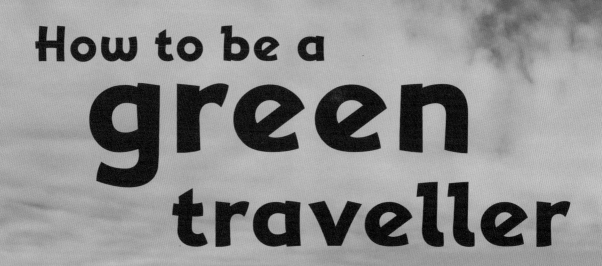

How to be a green traveller

The Blue Mountains National Park is one of the most popular tourist destinations in Australia, with almost four million visitors a year. Katherine Swarts lists the things that people can do there to reduce their impact.

Can you think of other things you can do to protect natural environments like the Blue Mountains? What are they?

The Blue Mountains

The Greater Blue Mountains World Heritage Area was the traditional homeland of six groups of Indigenous Australian Peoples. Visitors can see the first evidence of human occupation in the region during the Pleistocene glacial period, as well as rock art sites such as Red Hands Cave. Popular activities include bushwalking and camping, and there are many historic lookouts, picnic areas and walking tracks.

Although it has almost 270,000 hectares to explore, the many people who visit each year strain the park's ecosystem. When you visit the Blue Mountains, there are a lot of things you can do to help protect this important ecosystem.

Stay on well-travelled trails. Never take shortcuts — they damage the land by contributing to erosion. And some rare plants can take a hundred years to recover from being stepped on! Shortcuts can also lead you into dangerous places.

Never feed or try to touch wild animals, no matter how cute they may be. Human food is not good for wild animals, and too much of it can make them dependent on people.

Never pick plants or collect rocks. Many are rare or delicate. Doing so is against the law!

The area is home to 400 different species of animals, 40 of them rare or threatened. If you're lucky, you might see the elusive spotted-tailed quoll, which is listed as vulnerable.

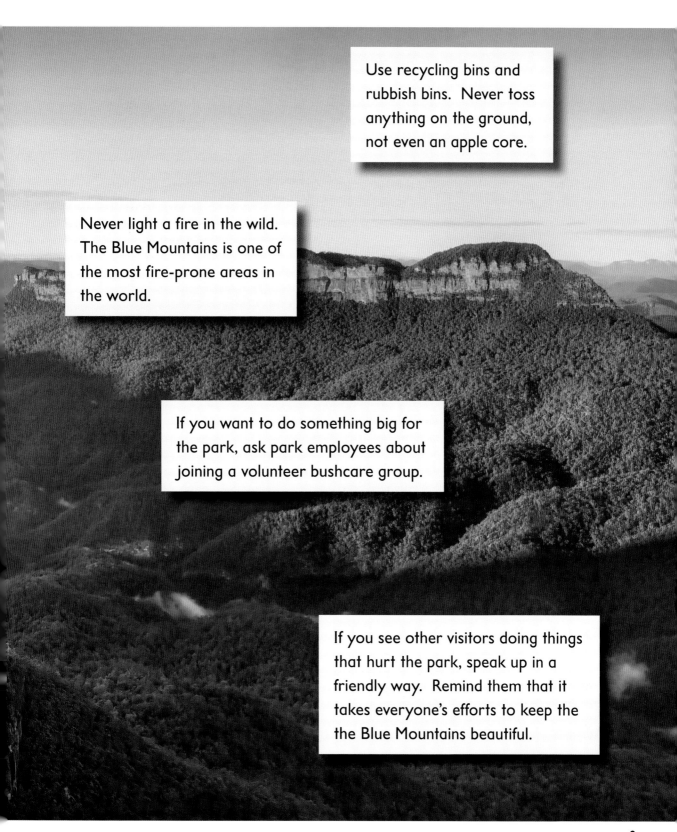

Use recycling bins and rubbish bins. Never toss anything on the ground, not even an apple core.

Never light a fire in the wild. The Blue Mountains is one of the most fire-prone areas in the world.

If you want to do something big for the park, ask park employees about joining a volunteer bushcare group.

If you see other visitors doing things that hurt the park, speak up in a friendly way. Remind them that it takes everyone's efforts to keep the the Blue Mountains beautiful.

The village from Frozen

In the mountains of Austria, there is a tiny village that looks like the kingdom of Arendelle from the popular movie *Frozen*. And because of the resemblance, this village is now inundated with tourists – one million people a year! As a result, life for the residents of Hallstatt has been greatly affected, writes Kerrie Shanahan.

The people who live in this village didn't ask for the tourists to come. What rights do we have to visit such tourist attractions? What responsibilities do we have?

Hallstatt, Austria

When people visit the tranquil village of Hallstatt, they are amazed by the beauty and history of this World Heritage site. But its popularity is causing problems for the 800 people who live there. They are completely outnumbered by strangers.

The tiny village is not equipped for this mass tourism. Many tourists arrive in Hallstatt on big buses that come and go all day every day. On busy days, there can be up to 90 buses in the village! The tourists are noisy and leave rubbish. They're also a drain on the water supply, using public bathrooms and drinking from water fountains.

The privacy of residents is threatened by overly curious tourists as they roam through the town. While exploring historic buildings, tourists have interrupted church services and even barged in on funerals. Security guards are now positioned outside the church to stop such intrusions. Traffic cones and Private Property signs are placed outside the homes of locals to discourage prying tourists from getting too close.

Some tourists spend money in the village when they visit and this is good for locals. Most tourists, however, are in the village for only a short time. They arrive on bus tours, take their photos and then leave.

So what can be done to protect this tiny community?

Tourists visit a vault behind a church in Hallstatt.

The people of Hallstatt are working on a plan that will make the most of the popularity of their village while also protecting it and ensuring the privacy of its residents.

The village hopes to reduce the amount of tourists that visit Hallstatt by 30 per cent. They also want visitors to stay longer so that they can spend some quality time in the town – and also spend some money.

The villagers' plan suggests that a maximum of 50 buses will be allowed to visit Hallstatt each day, and these buses must register with the Hallstatt tourism office before they arrive. Bus tours that spend more than a few hours in the village will be prioritised over others. This means tourists would be likely to spend more time and therefore more money in Hallstatt – eating in local restaurants, shopping, touring the salt mines or taking a boat cruise on the lake nearby. And this plan would be good for residents because it would generate more jobs.

But will this be enough to solve the problem? Will the locals once again enjoy their idyllic village with some privacy? Only time will tell if this story has a "happily-ever-after" ending.

At the beach

Look at these photos of beaches.

Which would *you* like to visit? Why?

My favourite holiday

Read about these students' favourite holidays.

What was your best holiday?
What did you like best about it?

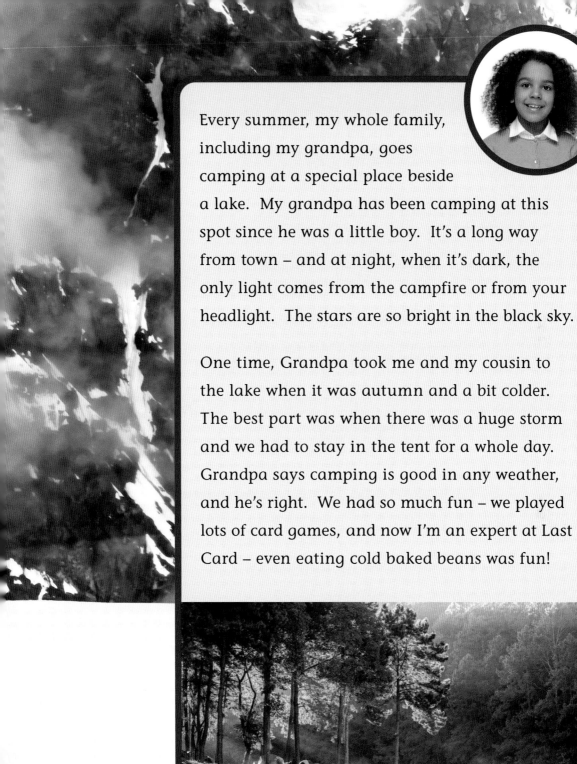

Every summer, my whole family, including my grandpa, goes camping at a special place beside a lake. My grandpa has been camping at this spot since he was a little boy. It's a long way from town – and at night, when it's dark, the only light comes from the campfire or from your headlight. The stars are so bright in the black sky.

One time, Grandpa took me and my cousin to the lake when it was autumn and a bit colder. The best part was when there was a huge storm and we had to stay in the tent for a whole day. Grandpa says camping is good in any weather, and he's right. We had so much fun – we played lots of card games, and now I'm an expert at Last Card – even eating cold baked beans was fun!

I like theme park holidays because they are lots of fun. But there are downsides. The crowds aren't great. If a little child wandered off, they would probably get lost. Adults get stressed over their kids getting lost. Another thing that I don't like is the long queues. The adults get bored and often think that the ride is a waste of time. Sometimes, you have to wait for hours. One final downside is the expense. Many theme park rides and the food are overpriced. I think theme parks should target all ages, not just kids.

My perfect holiday is going away to the beach. I really enjoy it because it is a tradition in my family and with family friends. I love going to the beach because it's not too crowded. There is plenty of room for everyone and it is very relaxing. I also like walking in the national park in the mornings with my family and friends.

One of my favourite things is going to the ice cream place next to the beach. I also love staying in the apartments. We all stay in the same apartments and visit each other. We also go to the swimming pool together.

My favourite holiday was when I went to Italy. I loved it because I got to meet lots of new people like my cousins who I had never met before, and my aunt and uncle. We didn't go out to eat. We ate with our aunt and uncle every day, and the food was so good. We were always with our family.

Every day was a new adventure. I saw lots of beautiful places that I never knew existed, like the Colosseum. It is 2,000 years old. I never knew that a building could stand for that long.

I bought a tin soldier from the Colosseum. It didn't cost very much. I bought it from a stall on the side of the road. I still have it in my bedroom. It reminds me of the best holiday I've had so far!

I live in a tourist attraction

Ally Adams lives in a small town by the sea. The town has a permanent population of about 1,100 people, but each summer, the number of people who visit while on holiday swells to over 13,000, writes Ally.

Is Ally right to complain about the summer visitors? How would you feel if you were Ally?

My town is small and beautiful. Tall forested hills surround it and the forest rolls down to the sea. About 1,100 people live in my town, but in summer during school holidays, there are about 13,000 residents. Do you think that changes the town? It certainly does!

The town is not easy to get to – you have to drive along a two-lane highway cut into a cliff. The road along the ocean is a tourist attraction in its own right, so from the very beginning of summer, there is a steady stream of cars travelling along the road.

That's the first sign that the tourist invasion has begun – a long line of cars, snaking into the town. *Go home,* I think. *Leave us with our quiet, peaceful little township.*

But I know that this is selfish of me. My parents own one of the local shops, and I know that during the winter months – when the tourists don't come – all of the people who run businesses have a very hard time. They all rely in some way on the tourists who come to stay for their summer holiday.

These tourists benefit our town. We would not have all of the facilities that the town can offer without the money that they bring. We wouldn't have our cinema. We wouldn't have as many restaurants. How would the supermarket survive without the summer season? The petrol station? The bookshop? The shop that sells delicious ice cream? The swimming pool and the skating park? Would we have our small but well-equipped hospital and our school? Of course not, and life would be much more difficult without all of these facilities.

I love the people who come to our camping ground every year. It's very close to the beach and a great place to stay. The families have a wonderful time, and they buy all of their food and anything else they need from our local shops. They contribute to our town.

But not all tourists are the same. There are tourists who give our town nothing. Close to our town, there is a dramatic gorge, and busloads of tourists come each summer just to take photos. The cliffs are steep, but there are railings to keep you from the edge and a long wooden stairway so that you can climb to the bottom, where there is a small beach. We love this gorge, but we know it's dangerous. There are lots of signs warning of the dangers.

But the tourists ignore these signs. They climb through the railings at the top of the cliff and take selfies. They don't even look at the gorge. Or they climb down the stairway a little and take more selfies. Then, they all get back on the bus and leave. They give us nothing!

I shouldn't complain. In reality, tourists make our town the great place that it is to live in – for the nine months of the year that they are not here!

What is your opinion? How to write a persuasive argument

1. State your opinion

Think about the issues related to your topic. What is your opinion?

2. Research

Research the information you need to support your opinion.

Related *Perspectives* book   Internet   Other sources

3. Make a plan

Introduction

How will you "hook" the reader?

State your opinion.

List reasons to support your opinion.

What persuasive devices will you use?

Reason 1
Support your reason
with evidence and details.

Reason 2
Support your reason
with evidence and details.

Reason 3
Support your reason
with evidence and details.

Conclusion

Restate your opinion. Leave your reader with a strong message.

4. Publish

Publish your persuasive argument.

Use visuals to reinforce your opinion.